19
of the Best and Most Beloved
Hymns & Spirituals

By Dick Sheridan

~oOo~

A diverse sampling of religious traditions

arranged for ukuleles in standard C tuning.

Adaptable to other chord and fretted instruments.

SBN 978-1-57424-295-9
SAN 683-8022

Cover by James Creative Group

CENTERSTREAM®

HALLELUJAH!

Definition: Hallelujah is an exclamation of worship or a call to praise transliterated from two Hebrew words meaning "Praise ye the Lord." Some Bible versions render the phrase "Praise the Lord." The Greek form of the word is alleluia.

Hallelujah in the Old Testament

Hallelujah is found 24 times in the Old Testament, but only in the book of Psalms. It appears in 15 different Psalms, between 104-150, and in almost every case at the opening and/or closing of the Psalm. These passages are called the "Hallelujah Psalms."

In Judaism, Psalms 113–118 are known as the Hallel, or Hymn of Praise. These verses are traditionally sung during the Passover Seder, Feast of Pentecost, Feast of Tabernacles, and the Feast of Dedication.

Hallelujah in the New Testament

In the New Testament the term appears exclusively in Revelation 19:1-6:

After this I heard what seemed to be the loud voice of a great multitude in heaven, crying out, "Hallelujah! Salvation and glory and power belong to our God, for his judgments are true and just; for he has judged the great prostitute who corrupted the earth with her immorality, and has avenged on her the blood of his servants."

Once more they cried out, "Hallelujah! The smoke from her goes up forever and ever."

And the twenty-four elders and the four living creatures fell down and worshiped God who was seated on the throne, saying, "Amen. Hallelujah!"

And from the throne came a voice saying, "Praise our God, all you his servants, you who fear him, small and great."

Then I heard what seemed to be the voice of a great multitude, like the roar of many waters and like the sound of mighty peals of thunder, crying out, "Hallelujah! For the Lord our God the Almighty reigns." (ESV)

Hallelujah at Christmas

Today, hallelujah is recognized as a Christmas word thanks to German composer George Frideric Handel (1685-1759). His timeless "Hallelujah Chorus" from the masterpiece oratorio Messiah has become one of the best-known and widely loved Christmas presentations of all time. Interestingly, during his 30 lifetime performances of Messiah, Handel conducted none of them at Christmas time. He considered it a Lenten piece. Even so, history and tradition altered the association, and now the inspiring echoes of "Hallelujah! Hallelujah!" are an integral part of the sounds of the Christmas season.

Pronunciation: hahl lay LOO yah

Hallelujah
Ukulele

* Includes solo

ABOUT THE AUTHOR

Dick Sheridan is no stranger to gospel music -- or to the ukulele. A product of parochial education, including a college with religious affiliation, he has sung with choirs and glee clubs, and is well familiar with the gospel repertoire. A regular church goer, he continues to enjoy hearing and singing the old traditional hymns as well as the more contemporary new ones.

Dick was reared by parents of different faiths, and as a result he feels he has a foot on both sides of the aisle. His parents' hymnals, along with his own, grace the family's music cabinet and top of the upright piano. Friends of various persuasions have introduced him to a wide range of their religious music. Even his Dixieland jazz band (with which he has played for over 40 years) includes numerous spirituals that lend themselves to that distinctive style and a host of worship services.

Ukuleles have been Dick's constant companion since childhood. First came a small soprano uke, then a larger baritone that he continues to play, and lately a tenor-size instrument on which the following songs were arranged.

In "Hallelujah Ukulele" you'll find a classic collection of hymns and spirituals that is sure to bring much enjoyment and satisfaction. The legacy of gospel music contained in this book lends itself readily to the ukulele. It has greatly enriched Dick's life, and he feels certain it will enrich yours too.

~oOo~

INTRODUCTION

Hymns and Spiritual songs have long been a part of our culture and faith traditions. From time immemorial they celebrate celestial glory, offer praise and thanksgiving, and provide enduring comfort throughout life's journeys. They commemorate the trials, travails and tribulations of bondage, slavery, and daily struggles, always with a message of hope and encouragement.

Thundering hymns echo from the world's great cathedrals and temples, while other places of worship – chapels, churches and synagogues – generally offer more sedate devotional music. Exuberant tent meetings and revivals resound with jubilant shouts and hollers. Even folk music can add a serious song or occasional light-hearted touch:

> *Cindy got religion, got it once before,*
> *Got so full of glory,*
> *shook her stockings to the floor.*

For many of us, Hymns and Spiritual songs have been a part of our lives since childhood. They come from worship services, Sunday school, Shabbat, prayer meetings, celebration of feasts and high holy days, family and social gatherings, and private devotion.

Enter the ukulele: Don't be surprised that many of these beautiful hymns and spirituals can be played on the ukulele as instrumentals or for vocal accompaniment. As the following collection will show, the many-faceted uke is capable of both the spirited and solemn. A bountiful harvest awaits. Play on! A world of fun, fulfillment and satisfaction beckons.

AMAZING GRACE

Ukulele tuning: gCEA

Traditional

AMAZING GRACE

once _____ was ___ lost, but now _____ am ___ found, was blind, but ___ now I see. _____

2. 'Twas grace that taught my heart to fear,
And grace my fears relieved.
How precious did that grace appear,
The hour I first believed.

3. When we've been here ten thousand years,
Bright shining as the sun,
We've no less days to sing God's praise
Than when we first begun.

ANGEL BAND

Ukulele tuning: gCEA

JEFFERSON HASCALL   WILLIAM B. BRADBURY

This beautiful hymn, now a cherished part of folk music, was taken from a poem written by Jefferson Hascall and set to music by William Bradbury in the early 1860s. It typically has been sung in rural and mountain areas by neighbors gathered outside the home of one whose life was known to be slipping away.

"Oh, come, Angel Band, come and around me stand ..."

2. I know I'm nearing holy ranks
   Of friends and kindred dear;
   I brush the dew of Jordan's banks,
   The crossing must be near.
      REFRAIN

3. I've almost gained my heav'nly home
   My spirit loudly sings;
   The holy ones, behold, they come!
   I hear the noise of wings.
      REFRAIN

GO DOWN, MOSES

Ukulele tuning: cGEA

Traditional

GO DOWN, MOSES

2. Thus saith the Lord, bold Moses said,
   "Let my people go!
   If not I'll smite your first-born dead,
   Let my people go!"
      CHORUS

3. "No more shall they in bondage toil,
   Let my people go!
   Let them come out with Egypt's spoil,
   Let me people go!"
      CHORUS

HIS EYE IS ON THE SPARROW

Ukulele tuning: gCEA

CIVILLA D. MARTIN

CHARLES H. GABRIEL

A young French student visited me for several summers. He loved Dixieland, and as it happened the Preservation Hall Jazz Band was in town during one of his stays. Because of a band engagement of my own, I was unable myself to take him to the concert, so I arranged for a friend to escort him. The next day I asked how he liked the concert. "Formidable!" he said. He especially enjoyed the song "His Eye Is On The Sparrow." Then he related a little story. His family was driving in their Citroen from Paris to a summer home in La Rochelle on the Brittany coast. The car had an open sunroof, and luggage was piled high on top of the car. Wham! The car hit a bird which tumbled through the sunroof. The young French boy slowly shook his finger at me and said, "I tell you, God He no have his eye and THAT sparrow!"

JUST A CLOSER WALK WITH THEE

Ukulele tuning: gCEA

Traditional

Verse: 1.I am weak but Thou art strong, Je - sus keep me from all wrong.

I'll be sa - tis fied as long_____ as I walk, let me walk close to Thee.

Refrain: Just a clos - er walk with Thee, grant it Je - sus is my plea,_____

Dai - ly walk-ing close to Thee,_____ let it be, dear Lord let it be.

HINE MAH TOV

(Pronounce: Hee Nay Ma Tove)

Ukulele tuning: gCEA

Traditional Hebrew

The inspiration for this song comes from
the opening words of Psalm 133 from the
Old Testament

Behold, how good it is, and how pleasant,
where brethren dwell at one.

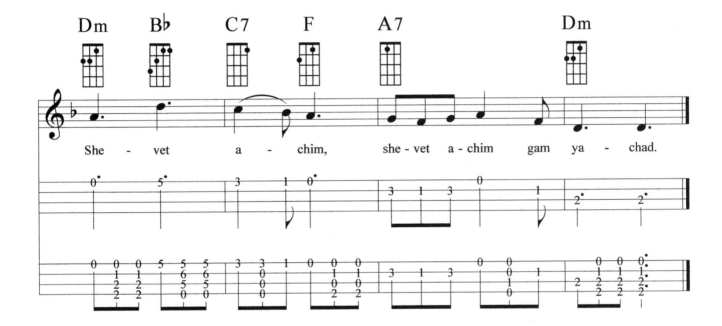

IN THE GARDEN

Ukulele tuning: gCEA

CHARLES A MILES

Verse: 1.I come to the gar-den a - lone,___ while the dew is still on the ros - es, and the voice I hear fall-ing on my ear the Son of God dis - clos - es. And He

Chorus: walks with me and He talks with me, and He tells me I am His own;___ and the joy we share as we tar - ry there, none oth-er has ev - er____ known.

2. He speaks and the sound of His voice
    Is so sweet the birds hush their singing,
    And the melody that He gave to me
    Within my heart is ringing.
        CHORUS

3. I'd stay in the garden with Him,
    Though the night around me is falling,
    But He bids me go, through the voice of woe
    His voice to me is calling.
        CHORUS

IN THE SWEET BY AND BY

Ukulele tuning: gCEA

JOSEPH P. WEBSTER

2. We shall sing on that beautiful shore,
   The melodious songs of the bless'd,
   And our spirits shall sorrow no more,
   Not a sigh for the blessing of rest.
   REFRAIN

3. To our bountiful Father above,
   We will offer our tribute of praise,
   For the glorious gift of His love,
   And the blessings that hallow our days.
   REFRAIN

17

OH, DEM GOLDEN SLIPPERS

Ukulele tuning: gCEA

JAMES A. BLAND

GOLDEN SLIPPERS

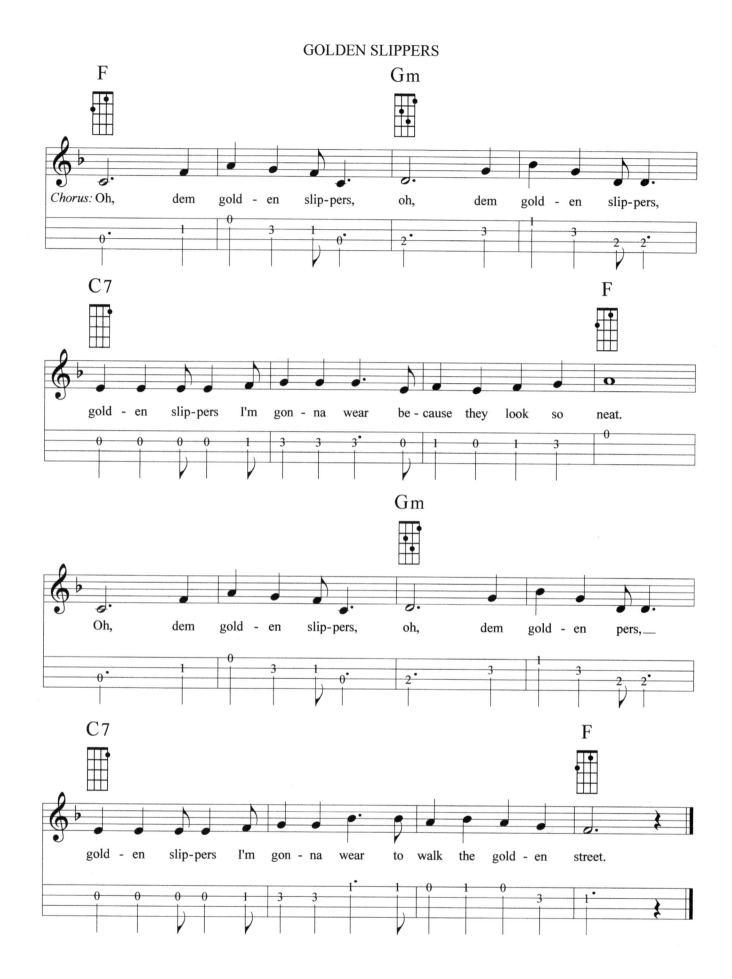

MICHAEL, ROW THE BOAT

Ukulele tuning: gCEA

Traditional

2. The river is deep and the river is wide -- milk and honey on the other side. CHORUS

3. Jordan's river is chilly and cold -- chills the body but not the soul. CHORUS

THE OLD RUGGED CROSS

Ukulele tuning: gCEA

GEORGE BENNARD

ROCK MY SOUL

Ukulele tuning: gCEA

Traditional

Rock my soul in the bo-som of A-bra-ham, rock my soul in the bo-som of A-bra-ham,

rock my soul in the bo-som of A-bra-ham, oh, rock-a my soul.

24

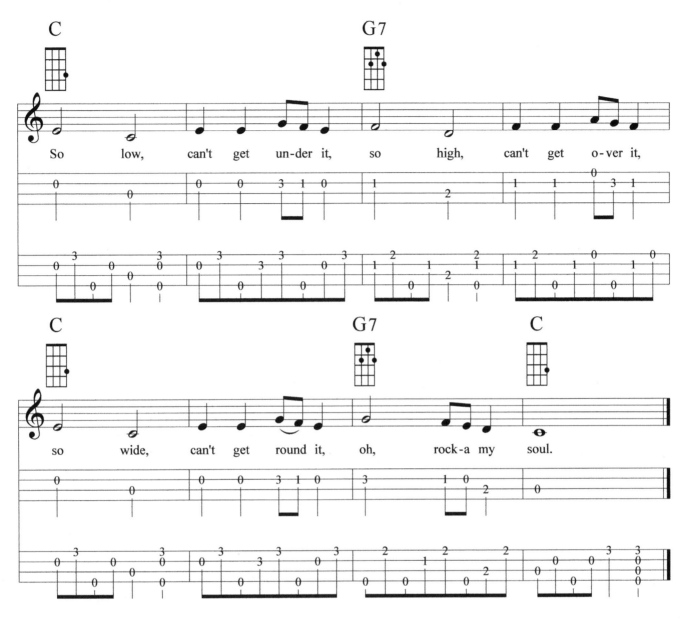

SHALL WE GATHER AT THE RIVER?

Ukulele tuning: gCEA

ROBERT LOWRY

2. On the margin of the river, washing up its silver spray,
   We will talk and worship ever, all the happy golden day.
   REFRAIN

3. Ere we reach the shining river, lay we every burden down,
   Grace our spirits will deliver, and provide a robe and crown.
   REFRAIN

4. At the smiling of the river, mirror of the Savior's face,
   Saints, whom death will never sever, lift their songs of saving grace.
   REFRAIN

5. Soon we'll reach the silver river, soon our pilgrimage will cease,
   Soon our happy hearts will quiver, with the melody of peace.
   REFRAIN

STANDING IN THE NEED OF PRAYER

Ukulele tuning: gCEA

Traditional

STANDING IN THE NEED OF PRAYER

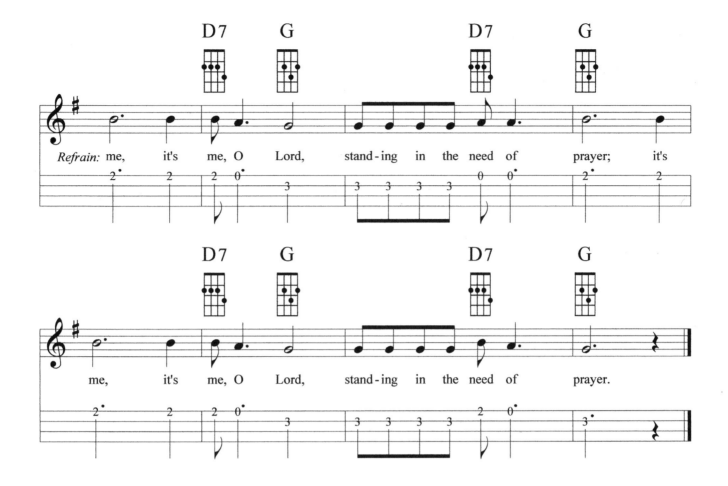

2. Not the parson, nor the deacon, but it's me, O Lord,
   Standing in the need of prayer;
   Not the parson, nor the deacon, but it's me, O Lord,
   Standing in the need of prayer.

3. Not my father, nor my mother, but it's me, O Lord,
   Standing in the need of prayer;
   Not my father, nor my mother, but it's me, O Lord,
   Standing in the need of prayer.

4. Not the stranger, nor my neighbor, but it's me, O Lord,
   Standing in the need of prayer;
   Not the stranger, nor my neighbor, but it's me, O Lord,
   Standing in the need of prayer.

SWING LOW, SWEET CHARIOT

Ukulele tuning: gCEA

WALLACE WILLIS

2. Sometimes I'm up, and sometimes I'm down,
    Coming for to carry me home,
    But still my soul feels heavenly bound,
    Coming for to carry me home.
        CHORUS

3. If I get there before you do,
    Coming for to carry me home,
    I'll cut a hole and pull you through,
    Coming for to carry me home.
        CHORUS

4. If you get there before I do,
    coming for to carry me home,
    Tell all my friends I'm coming too,
    Coming for to carry me home.
        CHORUS

THIS LITTLE LIGHT OF MINE

(DO, LORD)

Ukulele tuning: gCEA

Traditional

THIS LITTLE LIGHT OF MINE

THIS LITTLE LIGHT OF MINE

WHAT A FRIEND WE HAVE IN JESUS

Ukulele tuning: gCEA

JOSEPH M. SCRIVEN

CHARLES C. CONVERSE

WERE YOU THERE?

Ukulele tuning: gCEA

Traditional

WERE YOU THERE

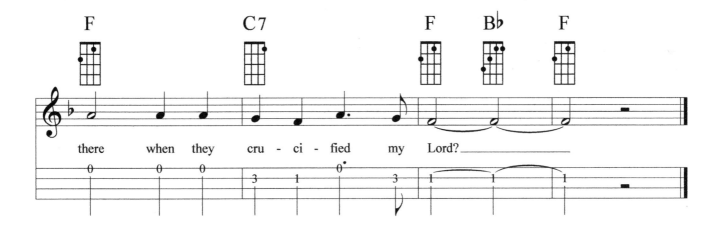

there   when   they   cru - ci - fied   my   Lord?_____

2. Were you there when they nailed Him to a tree?

3. Were you there when they pierced Him in the side?

4. Were you there when they laid Him in the tomb?

5. Were you there when they rolled away the stone?

WHEN THE SAINTS GO MARCHING IN

Ukulele tuning: gCEA

Traditional

WHEN THE SAINTS GO MARCHING IN

More Great Ukulele Books from Centerstream...